Henry Craske

A complete and authentic history of the campaign

Henry Craske

A complete and authentic history of the campaign

ISBN/EAN: 9783337150693

Printed in Europe, USA, Canada, Australia, Japan

Cover: Foto ©ninafisch / pixelio.de

More available books at **www.hansebooks.com**

THE HERO
OF THE
THIRTY-FOURTH.

ILLUSTRATED.

THE CITIZEN STEAM BOOK AND JOB PRINTING HOUSE, RUSHVILLE, ILL.

THE AUTHOR.

A COMPLETE AND AUTHENTIC

History of the Campaign

IN WHICH

"The Mighty Sleeper"

WAS DEFEATED

IN THE

34th Senatorial District of Illinois,

WHICH CULMINATED IN THE

Re-election of Hon. JOHN A. LOGAN

TO THE UNITED-STATES SENATE.

———

By HENRY CRASKE,

THE ORIGINATOR AND ORGANIZER

———OF———

"THE MOST DARING PIECE OF POLITICAL STRATEGY"

EVER CONCEIVED AND "SO SUCCESSFULLY EXECUTED
SINCE THE DAYS OF ALEXANDER THE GREAT."

———

PUBLISHED BY
ONE OF THE "FINE WORKERS,"
RUSHVILLE, ILLINOIS.
1885.

TO THAT MAN OF THE PEOPLE,

NOBLE PATRIOT, GRAND STATESMAN,

GALLANT GENERAL AND FRIEND OF THE SOLDIER,

JOHN A. LOGAN,

THIS LITTLE VOLUME IS

DEDICATED.

PREFACE.

At the earnest solicitation of many friends, who expressed a desire that a history be written of the memorable campaign which was fought to the end on the 6th day of May, 1885, in the Thirty-Fourth Senatorial District of Illinois (composed of the counties of Cass, Mason Menard and Schuyler), and which resulted in the election of a Republican to the Thirty-Fourth General Assembly, from a District that, in the Presidential campaign of 1884, gave a plurality of over 2,000 and a majority of nearly 1,800 for the Democratic electors; and believing so gallant a fight against such overwhelming odds was successful solely from the magnetizing and electrifying influence of the free use of the name of John A. Logan, the author has determined to present the facts in the best manner his humble ability will permit.

In collecting the facts for this little volume, the magnitude of the grand achievement has been more forcibly impressed upon me, showing the necessity of preserving a record of the events which led to the victory.

The belief that the people, generally, have a desire to learn the ways and means used to accomplish such a splendid result is the reason these pages have been written.

Trusting this little volume will meet the favor of a generous public, it is respectfully submitted by

THE AUTHOR.

CHAPTER I.

ORIGIN OF THE PLAN.

GENTLEMEN: According to promise, I will endeavor to write up for you a correct account of the plan and campaign by which a Republican was elected to fill the vacancy in the Thirty-Fourth General Assembly caused by the death of Representative J. Henry Shaw, of Beardstown, who died on the 12th of April, at the Leland hotel in Springfield.

In pursuance of law, the Governor, on April 13th, issued his proclamation calling a special election in the Thirty-Fourth Senatorial District for May 6th. On Wednesday, the 15th April, while thinking over the situation as developed from the fact that Representative Sittig had stated in the General Assembly that he was paired with Shaw until his successor shall have been elected, it occured to me that it would be a grand event for the Republican party, and a very great surprise to the Democratic party, and also to Representative Sittig, if a Republican should be elected to succeed Mr. Shaw. With this in view, I determined to write a plan and send it to General Logan to see what he thought of the project. I believed the Republicans of the State, and also the Republicans of the Nation, desired, above all things, that the Legislature of Illinois should elect to the United States Senate that gallant soldier, grand statesman, and man of the people, John A. Logan, the man who to-day is the central figure in American politics, and, undoubtedly, is the representative man of America. Believing this, and being inspired with the thought that it was possible to elect a Republican to the Legislature, thereby insuring the election of our candidate to the United States Senate, I wrote the following plan:

Original plan first sent to General Logan on April 16, 1885:

RUSHVILLE, ILL., April 16, 1885.

HON. JOHN A. LOGAN, Springfield, Ill.

Dear Sir: We, ex-members of the army, feel that in you the poor soldiers have a champion who will fight their cause, as perhaps no other man in this Nation can or will; and for this reason I submit a plan to you which I think, if properly worked, will turn the enemy's flank and put him to utter rout.

My plan is, for you to select a man in each county of the district, whom you know you can depend upon; he in turn to select a man in each school district; who in turn will select not more than five staunch Republicans whose duty it will be to see every true Republican in their district who can be depended on to keep it secret, and thus secure the attendance of all Republican voters at the polls at from three to five o'clock P. M., according to size of town or precinct; and with the apparent apathy that will seem to be in the Republican ranks, lulling the enemy into fancied security, thereby electing a Republican Representative.

My further plan is to have all the tickets printed at one office.

I suggest that you call a caucus to select the candidate for Representative from any county in the district outside of the county of Schuyler.

I refer you to Representative Logsdon as to who I am.

If you think this worthy of favorable consideration, I shall be pleased to assist, and endeavor to carry to a successful issue the result desired. I remain yours, very respectfully,

HENRY CRASKE.

I received the following letter from General Logan at twelve o'clock M., April 18th:

LELAND HOTEL, SPRINGFIELD, ILL., April 17, 1885.

Dear Sir: Your letter received and contents noted. I think your plan a good one and wish the Republicans in your district might go to work, in a quiet way, and elect a Republican.

Very respectfully,

JOHN A. LOGAN.

HENRY CRASKE, Rushville, Ill.

On Saturday, April 18th, the Hon. Perry Logsdon, of Rushville, Ill., Representative to the Thirty-Fourth General Assembly, came into my place of business. Of him I made the inquiry as to whether General Logan had said anything to him about a plan that I had forwarded on the 16th inst. Mr. Logsdon stated that he had not seen the General. I handed a copy of the plan to him. He read it through very carefully, being the first man to read it in my presence. When through reading it, I said to him, "What do you think of it?" He answered, "I think it an inspiration, and cannot help being a success, if there are no blunders made in its execution." I told him that I thought it would take some money to carry the plan out successfully, as it would require time to explain it, and a great deal of special effort to induce the Republican voters to come out and vote on the 6th. Their hopeless minority made it seem an impossibility for them to be victorious in this Senatorial District.

Mr. Logsdon promised his assistance and hearty co-operation in carrying forward the plan to a successful issue.

On the evening of the 18th, W. I. Larash, of Rushville, editor of *The Schuyler Citizen,* was handed a copy of the plan which had been sent General Logan. He was asked to read it and give me his opinion of it, he being the second person who had read the plan in my presence. He stated that if it could be worked successfully it would convulse the Nation.

I then showed him the letter from General Logan, dated April 17. We read the letter, considered it in all its bearings, and talked over the selection of the men to act as township committeemen. We felt that the grand result was almost accomplished. Mr. Larash said that the Democrats would say: "It was a d—d dirty trick."

Then doubts would come over the spirit of our dream. We read the subject matter over again and agreed that it looked fine on paper. We again became enthusiastic. As our meeting had lasted till a very late hour, it being nearly Sunday morning, we agreed to adjourn.

On Monday, the 20th of April, I invited the Rev. Fletcher M. Sisson, pastor of the First M. E. Church, into my room, and read the plan; also read General Logan's letter, withholding the name. He was asked what he thought of the plan, and of the letter. He said he thought the plan was a good one, and it would be a grand good thing if it should prove a success.

I then told him the plan had been sent to John A. Logan, and the letter read was his answer. He stated that the letter showed very plainly that the General had not much faith that the plan could be successfully carried out; but still was willing to encourage the effort by approving the plan. The more Rev. Sisson thought of it, the more enthusiastic he became. This was very encouraging.

I expected to hear something further from General Logan. In the meantime it was very hard to possess myself with patience. The whole matter was discussed a great many times with W. A. Crosier, of Rushville, and it was agreed between us, that we would discourage any talk that suggested the possibility of carrying the district. We found several men who wanted to talk about the possibility of such a thing, which suggestion we of course discouraged at once.

CHAPTER II.

ORGANIZING IN SCHUYLER.

On Friday, the 24th of April, I asked Mr. Crosier if he would not like to read the plan, and also General Logan's letter in answer to same. After reading them, he felt with me, that the General would certainly make some further move in the matter soon. In the mean time I determined to see the men who would do good and efficient work in their respective townships, and the following were selected:

E. M. Bradley, for Frederick; Sherman B. Dray, for Browning; George W. Ware, for Hickory; Peter Phillips, for Oakland; Wm. C. Thompson (who called to his assistance Dr. Lewis C. Seeley), for Littleton; Jerome Pettijohn, for Huntsville; Charles Phelps and George H. Wier, for Birmingham; Major Robert Blackburn and Alexander M. Prather, for Brooklyn; Capt Robert A. Williams, L. P. Allphin, and John A. Points, for Camden; Martin G. Rice, D. E. Ray, W. B. Ray, Robert McCreery, Wm. Harman and Ed. DeWitt, for Buenavista; Charles W. Davis and Abraham Lamaster, for Bainbridge. Hon. Perry Logsdon agreed, with the assistance of Samuel Lashbrook, to work Woodstock; Leander Kennedy, Wm. Tremble, George W. Bellomy, W. W. Potts, Wm. Ramsey, and George W. Barnhart, for Rushville.

After making the selection, I determined to see and give instructions to those living in distant townships first. The first man instructed was E. M. Bradley, of Frederick. He was enthused all over and fell readily into the work. The next man was Sherman B. Dray, of Browning. He also thought it was a good thing and promised his hearty co-operation. The third man was that old wheel-horse of the Republican party, Jerome Pettijohn, of Huntsville, who got so enthusiatic over the matter that he could not stay at home, but had to spend a week in Rushville awaiting developments.

On Monday, the 27th of April, the Hon. R. W. Mills, of Virginia, Cass county, came to Rushville to attend court. He called on me in the evening and during the conversation that followed, I asked him if he did not think we could do something to help out our candidate for the United-States Senate, and secure his election. He replied that he saw no other way than to make a "still hunt" and elect a Republican to succeed Shaw. I then told him of the plan, and its details, that had been sent to General Logan; and also of the General's reply. He was also informed of my waiting for something further from Springfield; as it seemed to me an old campaigner like the General, would certainly understand that it would take some money to pay the men who would be engaged in getting the vote out. Mr. Mills agreed with me that it would take about two hundred and fifty dollars for each county; in all about one thousand dollars.

It was my determination to make the effort to carry the district whether the money was raised or not, believing that each county would be willing to defray its own expense, and wrote the following plan, of which I forwarded a copy to Capt. S. H. Blaine, of Petersburg, Menard county; and to Capt. Samuel Bivens, of Havana, Mason county:

RUSHVILLE, ILL., April 28, 1885.

Dear Sir: Herewith I send you plan which I think, if properly worked, would elect a Republican Representative in the Thirty-Fourth Senatorial District.

It is this: That one man be selected in each county to manage said county, he in turn to select one man in each township of the county, he in turn to select one man in each school district, who in turn, will select five others to assist him.

All engaged in this work being as secret as the grave. All to start out on the morning of the 6th to see that all Republicans are at their respective voting places, promptly at 4 o'clock P. M., thereby insuring the election of a Republican Representative.

Results to follow this: First, the re-organization of the House; Second, the election of John A. Logan; Third, the great satisfaction which will pervade the Republican ranks, thereby making it possible to have a better organization in the party throughout the State.

I think we ought to strain every nerve to accomplish such a grand result. Yours, to command,   HENRY CRASKE.

I also sent the same plan to Representative Logsdon with this addition:—

In order to carry this to a successful issue it will be necessary to raise one thousand dollars out side of the four counties. I think, in fact I know, that two hundred and fifty dollars carefully used in each county would come near getting out the Republican vote.

If you think it prudent, would like to have you show this to some of your colleagues in the House. Of course prompt action must be taken on this if acted on at all.

After a candidate is selected, tickets to be printed at one office.

R. W. Mills wrote a note to Capt. Blaine, stating that he was appointed to manage his county, also stating that he nominated him (Blaine) for Representative. This note was placed in the envelope with the plan and forwarded to its destination.

Mr. Mills also wrote a note to Capt. Bivens, notifying him that he (Bivens) was selected to manage Mason county. He also wrote on the margin of plan which was sent to Logsdon:

"I believe we can win if we get the funds. The Democrats are not enthusiastic over their man."

This plan and instructions were mailed on the morning of the 28th of April. Mr. Mills agreed to manage his county with the aid of Hon. F. M. Davis, of Beardstown. On the 29th, I received the following letter from the Hon. Perry Logsdon:

SPRINGFIELD, ILL., April 28, 1885.

HENRY CRASKE, Rushville, Ill.

My Dear Sir: There is a gentleman here from Virginia to see me in reference to the same matter you wrote to J. A. L. I think there will be some one to see you before many days. If anything is done it must be done at once.

This man (Lancaster) thinks this may be worked successfully, and be the means of sending J. A. L. to U. S. S.

Respectfully yours, PERRY LOGSDON.

On the 30th of April, the following letter was received from Mr. Logsdon:

SPRINGFIELD, ILL., April 29, 1885.

Mr. HENRY CRASKE, Rushville, Ill.

Dear Sir: Since I wrote you yesterday, a caucus was held in General L.'s room, by some men of our district, Jacob Wheeler and Dan Shepard. Your plan was discussed and thought to be a good one. There will be some of our men in Capital to-morrow, who will then determine on some one for a candidate.

I write this morning so you may know what to depend on; and

lay your plans accordingly. I will be in Rushville on Saturday. Hope to see you.   Very truly yours,

PERRY LOGSDON.

Upon receipt of this letter, I determined to see all the men that were selected to organize the townships as soon as possible. Our circuit court being in session, Judge Matthews presiding, gave me a splendid opportunity to see all of the men especially entrusted with the work, and to give them full and complete instructions. Among other things, the following printed circular, gotten up with the assistance of W. A. Crosier and the editor of *The Citizen,* was handed to committeemen in Schuyler county:

CIRCULAR.

PLAN FOR TOWNSHIP COMMITTEEMAN.

FIRST. To select a man in each school district, that you *know* will carry out this plan with fidelity and strict secrecy. You are to distribute the tickets, through him, to every Republican voter in each school district. You to have the general supervision of the same.

DUTY OF SCHOOL-DISTRICT COMMITTEEMAN.

FIRST. To appoint not more than five voters who can be relied upon to assist in the distribution of tickets not earlier than the night before the election.

SECOND. The committeeman will, before exposing this plan, obtain a pledge, upon the voter's honor, to secrecy; and obtain, if possible, his faithful promise to be at the voting place promptly at 5 o'clock in the evening, on the day of election.

Particular attention was given to the fact that no voting should be done until 5 o'clock. I also notified them that I expected the tickets here on Saturday, May 2d, and requested all those remaining in town on that day to call at 2 o'clock P. M., receive the tickets and take them to their several townships for distribution.

On Friday evening, May 1st, I received the following letter from Captain Bivens:

HAVANA, ILL., April 30, 1885.

Messrs. CRASKE and MILLS:

Gents: I am in receipt of your communication of the 28th inst. and will say, I think your plan a good one; but as it is my busy season collecting taxes, I can not possibly do the work you assign to me, but would suggest the name of Prof. D. M. Blair, county superintendent of schools, as a very suitable man, and a very zealous worker in the Republican cause. I think he will (if solicited) take hold of the matter and do good work. Very truly yours,

SAMUEL BIVENS.

Accompanying this was a short note from Mr. Mills, in which he says:

I saw Col. Judy's son, of Menard, to-day. He said, "Dan. Shepard had written the Col. to meet them in Springfield, yesterday." I also saw Cleaveland, Representative from Rock Island. He approved of plan and said he would see to having the money raised.

We are organized here and ready for the fight.

Yours truly, R. W. MILLS.

On the morning of May 2d, I sent the following letter to Mr. Mills, at Virginia.

RUSHVILLE, ILL., May 2, 1885.

Dear Sir: Your favor received in connection with Captain Bivens' letter. Would say that we are thoroughly organized here and conversant with the fact that there was a meeting held at Springfield day before yesterday; but do not know the result, only that everything was lovely.

You must put Prof. D. M. Blair at work at once in Mason. As you see, Bivens declines to work. For God's sake and J. A. L.'s

sake and the sake of the Republican party in the State, don't
fail on this.   Very truly yours,

HENRY CRASKE.

R. W. MILLS, Virginia, Ill.

On Saturday, about 10 o'clock, A. M., the Hon. Perry
Logsdon called on me. He told me he left Springfield
Thursday evening, and that Mr. Beekman, of Menard
county, had been selected as the candidate; that Capt.
Blaine had been spoken of, but he being State's
Attorney, it was thought best to put some one else on
the ticket; therefore Beekman was selected. He also
said General Logan told him the tickets should be
shipped to Rushville, to arrive Saturday; and that
Mr. Beekman was the man.

The tickets failed to arrive on Saturday on either of
the trains. We have only two trains each day. One
arrives at 12, M., the other at 4, P. M. Mr. Logsdon
gave me an order on the express company, in case the
tickets were addressed to him. I waited until both
trains had arrived, but tickets did not come. I then
wired Capt. S. H. Blaine, at Petersburg, Menard
county, the following:

Have you received your goods yet? Mine have not arrived.
Please answer.

I waited till about 7 o'clock, P. M., for an answer.
I then made up my mind it would be best to have
tickets printed at *The Citizen* office, sufficient for this
county; but when I tried to learn Mr. Beekman's
christian name, there was not a man among us who was
able to tell me with certainty. I now asked Wm. A.
Crosier to go to Beardstown in the morning to see the
Hon. F. M. Davis to learn Mr. Beekman's christian
name, so the tickets could be printed and distributed

Monday. He said he thought it would be unwise for him to go, as the Democrats would suspect something. It was then agreed that he should see Judge A. C. Matthews, and tell him that I wished to see him on special business. Mr. Crosier soon came back with Judge Matthews. I knew the Judge was an ardent Republican and staunch supporter of Logan, and believed he would be willing to sacrifice himself for one day. I therefore explained the whole plan to him and asked him to go to Beardstown Sunday morning. He said, "Use me in any place and manner that you please to accomplish such a glorious result as the election of John A. Logan to the United States Senate." We agreed to start at 7 o'clock, A.M. A carriage and team were ordered to be at the Judge's hotel promptly at 7 in the morning, with a good Republican driver. To an outsider, our purpose appeared to be to fix up some fences for the Judge, as he thought of being a candidate before the Non-partisan Judicial Convention, called to meet at Mt. Sterling on June 7th.

The carriage and driver, Mr. John Potts, the Judge and myself were promptly on time Sunday morning. Like old campaigners, in order that our destination should be unknown, we made a detour in a direction opposite the one in which we wished to go. In an hour and a half we reached Frederick, where we met that staunch old "wheel-horse" and "true-blue" Republican, Grove Coningham, Sr., who invited us to his house to rest ourselves. We informed him that we wanted his boat and a good, true Republican to take us to Beardstown. The Judge also stated that he was around looking after his fences a little, as well as other matters.

Mr. Coningham agreed to get us a good, trusty man. On starting to the boat we inquired where the man was, who was to row us down. Mr. Coningham said he would be along presently. We got in the boat, and were surprised to find that Mr. Coningham, though well into the seventies, was the man. We made the trip down in about one hour and a half, there being a stiff wind up stream. On arrival, we called on Mr. Davis, to whom we explained our visit and found, much to my surprise, that he had heard nothing of the plan. We explained the whole matter to him and gave him a few of the printed plans for township and school-district committeemen. Having given him the necessary instructions, and having obtained from him the candidate's full name, John T. Beekman, we returned to Frederick on the steamer Calhoun. (I have since been very glad that we went to Beardstown, as it gave a majority for the Republican ticket of eighty; the usual majority being about sixty-six the other way).

We arrived at Frederick about 11 o'clock, A.M., meeting there George W. Ware, of Sheldons Grove, E. M. Bradley, John B. Hinton, and others, who were very much pleased to meet Judge Matthews. We also met Dr. D. C. Linn, an old college-mate of the Judge. The affable and gentlemanly officers of the Calhoun made the Judge a present of some early vegetables which were served on Mrs. Coningham's table for dinner; after which Grove and his accomplished daughter, Bessie, treated us to some very choice selections of vocal and instrumental music.

About 1 o'clock, P. M., E. M. Bradley and John B. Hinton called according to previous agreement. The plan and its details were then explained to Mr. Coningham and Mr. Hinton, the latter having learned something about it from Mr. Bradley. Grove remarked, "Well! I thought there was something besides this judicial business on deck." It was agreed that Mr. Hinton should come to Rushville and get the tickets for Frederick, Browning, and Hickory townships, and that Mr. Bradley should deliver them to Browning and Hickory. Having spent a very pleasant day, we returned to Rushville, unexpectedly meeting on our way home, the Democratic Senator from the Thirty-Fourth District, Hon. J. Munroe Darnell, in company with that staunch Republican, George E. Hall, of Rushville. We greeted them very cheerily and passed on, wondering whether the honorable senator would suspect anything, it being so near election day.

Upon our arrival home, I received a telegram from Capt. Blaine, in reply to mine of the day before, stating:

"I have received my goods. Yours were shipped Saturday, will arrive Monday."

I, therefore, expected certainly that the tickets would be on hand at 12 o'clock, Monday noon.

CHAPTER III.

A CLOSE CALL.

On Monday morning, we were all in fine shape, and the men who were to make the deliveries had everything in readiness to start. But I was again sorely disappointed by the non-arrival of the tickets and concluded to have them printed for the county at *The Citizen* office. I therefore stepped over to Mr. Larash's office and told him that owing to the emergency, he must print the following tickets, at once, as none had arrived so far, and men were waiting to take them to the distant parts of the county:

For Representative Thirty-Fourth
Senatorial District.
JOHN T. BEEKMAN.

Larash being a practical printer, did the printing himself, but was greatly hindered by an unusual number of suspicious appearing Democrats, who seemed to be unusually familiar, causing him to leave the press a number of times, thereby delaying the tickets several hours. This, however, in the end, proved to be a God-send, as the delay prevented my sending out to more than five townships before the 4 o'clock freight train came in, bringing the long-looked-for package of tickets, which was delivered at my store by the genial and accommodating railroad agent, Martin G. Rice. To my great surprise and consternation the tickets read:

"For Representative to General
Assembly,

W. H. WEAVER."

showing plainly that a mistake or change had been made. This was evidence of approaching danger, and soldier-like, we at once set to work to rectify the trouble. Mr. Rice helped arrange tickets in small lots and place them in envelopes for distribution to the townships.

Wm. A. Crosier had started for Huntsville, Birmingham, and Brooklyn townships, intending to make his quarters for the night at Jerome Pettijohn's, near Huntsville, twenty miles from Rushville. George W. Barnhart had started for Littleton and Oakland townships, intending to stop over night at Samuel Ellis'. Both had started with the Beekman tickets, and the great thing to do now was to find men who could be trusted, and would be willing to ride that distance as quickly as the emergency demanded. Robert McCreery was signaled to follow me to the livery stable. I found at the stable, John Potts, proprietor, and Hinman Munroe, a grocer. These gentlemen were told that two men were wanted, one to ride to Huntsville, the other to Littleton and Oakland as fast as horse-flesh could carry them. Mr. McCreery said it would kill him to ride that distance. The other gentlemen said they were willing to do the riding if they knew what it was for. They were told that it rested with them whether or not John A. Logan should be elected to the United States Senate. A brief explanation was given them. I handed the gentlemen the Weaver tickets, and they immediately started on their mission, which they successfully performed. Mr. Potts afterward remarked that he did so at the serious loss of the cuticle from that part of his body that came in contact with the saddle; he will be an applicant for a pension for wounds received while engaged in meritorious service.

Little did those gentlemen realize how nearly they came to defeating the grand object by changing candidates and by delay in forwarding the tickets. At this time I was in the most nervous condition of my life, knowing that the mighty stakes for which we were playing, might be lost on account of this miserable mistake, but made up my mind to remedy it if it was possible to do so.

John B. Hinton, of Frederick, called and received the tickets for the three townships that he had agreed to supply. Martin G. Rice had taken the tickets for Buenavista township. Walter B. Nell, of Rushville, agreed to start at daybreak and deliver the tickets to Charles W. Davis, of Bainbridge, and Perry Logsdon, of Woodstock. Mr. Logsdon was greatly surprised at the change of candidate but concluded it was all right; yet could not see why he had not been informed of the change.

CHAPTER IV.

A JUDICIOUS MOVE.

By agreement of some of the Republicans in the town and county, it had been arranged to call a meeting for Monday, May 4th, to select delegates to attend the Non-partisan Judicial Convention at Mt. Sterling, on Thursday, May 7th; but owing to unavoidable circumstances, the call was issued for Tuesday, the 5th, to meet at lawyer Mann's office. As will soon appear, this proved very fortunate for those engaged in carrying forward the grand work of electing a Republican Representative.

On Monday night, William Trimble and Leander Kennedy came in for tickets. They also took some to George W. Bellomy. Early Tuesday morning, George Montooth got tickets for Oakland township, and was notified that two hundred had already been sent to Peter Phillips.

As time rolled on, and the nearer the eventful day approached, the more anxious we became; for it seemed to us the Democrats were growing very suspicious. We supposed their suspicions were aroused by seeing numerous groups of active workers of the Republican party consulting on the street. We, therefore, resolved that we would not stop on the street to talk on any subject, until the 6th of May had passed; for we noticed the Democrats, in groups, very earnestly engaged in discussing some project unknown to us. For the purpose of throwing them off their guard, the call for the Judicial Convention furnished the necessary lever.

The Non-partisan Convention, to meet at Mt. Sterling, May 7th, was for the purpose of taking into consideration the expediency of making nominations for judges in this (sixth) judicial circuit. We had agreed, in the meantime, that it would be unwise for Schuyler to be represented in any way that would injure Judge Tunnicliff, he being an independent candidate for the Supreme Bench in this district. After thinking the matter over and learning more in regard to the proposed convention, it was decided that a caucus should be called to meet, as before mentioned, at the office of P. E. Mann, to select delegates. There being no opportunity to make the call through the papers, it was issued through the postoffice. Owing to the press of business, the editor of *The Citizen* did not have time to print the call until Tuesday, the 5th. The time appointed was 1 o'clock of that day. This proved to be a lucky delay for the Republicans, and as Mr. Larash stated, it would disarm whatever suspicions were held by our Democratic friends. We were also very careful to let it leak out that we were opposed to the regular Democratic nominee for Circuit Judge, John C. Bagby.

Promptly at 1 o'clock, as per call, a number of Republicans appeared at the office before mentioned. We then learned that Mr. Mann was absent on business, and adjourned to the office of Dr. John

A. Harvey. This movement created quite a stir among the Democrats and other citizens who had not "caught on." The excitement ran high on both sides. But the sturdy Republicans moved gracefully through the ordeal without evolving a scintillation of their real object.

The meeting was composed of the following gentlemen: John A. Points, of Camden; Wm. A. Crosier, of Buenavista; George W. Barnhart, Dr. John A. Harvey, of Rushville; and the author. Dr. Harvey was elected chairman and George W. Barnhart, secretary. W. B. Nell, Wm. A. Crosier, W. I. Larash, and H. Craske were appointed delegates to the Non-partisan Judicial Convention at Mt. Sterling.

PUTTING A DEMOCRAT IN REPUBLICAN HARNESS.

Dr. T. H. Downing, the skillful dental physician of Rushville, who is a staunch and active Democrat, occupies two rooms in the rear of the same building in which this caucus was held. The doors of his rooms were open and the dentist, presumably, engaged at his work. After the credentials were made out and signed and the proceedings reduced to writing, on motion of W. I. Larash, who had just stepped into the office, the minutes of the meeting were read in a very loud tone so that the worthy dentist might hear all that had been done. On motion, the caucus adjourned without day.

The presence of the Democrat worked splendidly, for the caucus had no sooner adjourned than Dr. Downing sounded the alarm all along the lines. He was not a very warm supporter of the entire Democratic Judicial ticket, and, while he took a great deal of comfort from the movement, he, at the same time, stirred up Bagby's friends, who naturally construed the action of the Republicans as a direct thrust at Judge Bagby. This was just what we desired above all things, as it effectually threw them off the track as to our *real* object.

It is said by the Democrats that on Tuesday, about 4 or 5 o'clock, P. M., Judge Bagby received a telegram from Hon. Scott Wyke, stating, "We hear rumors of movement to beat Leeper. Sound the alarm." Many Democrats and some Democratic papers subsequently claimed that Judge Bagby failed to "sound the alarm," and that he, indirectly, aided in electing a Republican to succeed Shaw; but Republicans who were conversant with the facts believe that the action of Tuesday's caucus threw the Judge and his friends here completely off their guard. They undoubtedly thought that Judge Matthews' trip on Sunday and the caucus held on Tuesday were in harmony with each other. It has been stated that S. B. Montgomery received a telegram on Monday, May 4th, from Senator Darnell saying, "The boys in Virginia are alarmed. Attend to it at once." Notwithstanding this, Mr. Montgomery's Democracy has never been questioned, nor need it be, I am satisfied that Judge Bagby and S. B. Montgomery believed the telegrams were simply for the purpose of getting out a larger Democratic vote, so as to show that the party was not asleep, and for this reason they did not exert themselves as they would have done had they suspected the facts in the case. It, however, was a surprise to Republicans, that old campaigners.

like the gentlemen above mentioned, suffered their forces to go to sleep in the face of a vigilant enemy.

It must be remembered that the Republicans, if they followed instructions, had the hard work to do on Tuesday night and Wednesday morning;—that of interviewing the voters, distributing tickets, explaining the situation, and obtaining their promise not to say anything to any one, and, also, not to vote before 5 o'clock, P. M. And "as fortune favors the brave," a heavy rain storm came up Tuesday night which tried the mettle of the special workers in the great cause; but they proved equal to the occasion and did splendid work, as the result next day plainly demonstrated.

Wednesday morning, the 6th of May, dawned bright and clear, which the Republicans believed was a favorable augury for their success. In Rushville, all was quiet as a summer day. The Democrats were apparently quiet, as if they were satisfied that no disturbing forces were at work. This continued until 10 o'clock, A. M., when unusual activity ruled among the Democrats who were in sight. Saddle-horses, teams, buggies, and carriages were hastily secured and might have been seen leaving town with prominent Democrats, riding and driving at break-neck speed; also as soon as a Democrat came in from the country he was sent back post haste, with instructions to rally the voters, as the Republicans were going to run in a "cold deck" late in the day. This flurry was all caused, as we afterwards learned, by a prominent Democratic-Greenback-Republican-Democrat, of Bainbridge township, who told Mark Bogue, the Democratic county clerk, that a Republican had said to him the evening of the 5th that the Republicans were going to have a candidate and do their voting late in the day. We knew from their movements that they had learned something, but believing that our organization was perfect, if instructions were followed, we felt confident of success. We also believed that, on such short notice, it would be impossible for the Democrats to rally their men in sufficient numbers to overcome our organization. It has been learned since the election, that on Monday, May 4th, the following "moss-backs," namely, Mark Bogue, S. B. Montgomery, and Wm. Bader, met in the office of the Rushville *Times,* the Democratic organ of the county, edited by Edwin Dyson, who was also present. Bader, Montgomery, and Bogue urged the necessity of sending a circular letter to the Democrats in the county warning them of danger, and urging them to vote on the 6th, as it was possible that the Republicans would undertake quietly to run a candidate, and defeat the Democratic nominee, thus bringing about a terrible state of affairs. Mr. Dyson considered this step altogether unnecessary, as he did not believe the Republicans would attempt such a thing. The circulars were not sent out, and thus the only means that might have defeated the Republicans was neglected, to the everlasting regret of the four gentlemen who discussed the project and then abandoned it.

As the day wore on, the Republicans, eager and expectant, gathered in town, apparently oblivious of the fact that it was election day, but in reality burning with impatience, awaiting the time to deposit their ballots in conformity with the plan. At last the critical hour arrived and they commenced voting and kept up a continuous stream of Republican votes until the polls closed.

I know of three Democrats who voted for the Republican candidate. One of them said to me, "Give me one of your tickets. I am tired of this farce at Springfield." Another said, "I want to vote the Republican ticket to end the 'dead-lock', and elect a U. S. Senator." Still another being in doubt, when asked if he desired to see matters settled in Springfield, a United States Senator elected, and the State saved two thousand dollars per day, concluded, in a spirit of economy, to vote the Republican ticket.

Early in the day, a few patriotic and impulsive Republicans who were not posted in the matter and who believe in exercising the right to vote whenever opportunity offers, voted the Democratic ticket.

An event showing quick appreciation of all surroundings occurred at the Rushville polls. Several Republicans were in the room, and were hesitating as to whether they should vote. They did not know the Republicans had a candidate, and were about to vote the Democratic ticket. Dr. J. H. Ewing, one of the clerks of the board, promptly suggested that they vote for John Putman, an ardent Republican, formerly a resident of Rushville, now "an offensive partisan" living at Beardstown, Cass county. This served somewhat to weaken the suspicions of the Democratic strikers who were hovering around the polls and closely scanning every Republican who happened to stroll that way.

John McCabe, of Rushville, deserves great credit

for effective work in notifying Republican voters, and getting them to the polls in the "nick of time."

To J. N. Roach, the author will ever feel grateful for the words of encouragement and approval which he gave during the organization.

Many amusing incidents occurred and mistakes were made during the day. For instance, while talking to a Democrat a Republican came to me and said in a loud voice, "Say! let me have some of those tickets." As good fortune would have it, a concert was billed for the evening of the 6th. I said to him: "I only secured two tickets, but go to Crosier & Hutton's marble shop. They have tickets more than they need." He seemed to take the hint and left. Again, a Republican and a Democrat were engaged in conversation. The Democrat handed the Republican a ticket and asked him if he would not vote it. He replied that he did not think he would, and the Democrat walked away. Another Republican, seeing the Democratic ticket, said in a loud voice, "I've got a different kind of a ticket from that." Fortunately the Democrat did not notice what was said, and passed on. Such incidents were very trying to the nerves, in spite of their amusement.

On Thursday morning, May 7th, W. A. Crosier, W. B. Nell, W. I. Larash, and the author started for Mt. Sterling, at 7 o'clock, A. M., to attend the Judicial Convention. We obeyed the stern behests of duty on this occasion, much against our inclination, as we would have preferred very much to remain at home to learn the result of the election. We arrived in Mt. Sterling about 10 o'clock, A. M., and there learned that it was rumored that the Republicans had carried the Thirty-Fourth District. At 2 o'clock, P. M., a telegram was received from Maj. W. H. Brackenridge, Representative from the Thirty-Sixth District, at Springfield, stating, "From all that I can learn, a Republican will succeed Shaw." This was very gratifying indeed, to those of us who lived in the Thirty-Fourth.

After resolving that it was inexpedient to make nominations, the convention adjourned. After a drive of about three hours, we reached home. Just as we entered town, we met Dr. John A. Harvey, who informed us that the Republicans had carried the county by one hundred and sixty-one majority, and that the Democrats were very sick. This was like an exhilirating beverage to us.

Before leaving home in the morning, I had commissioned M. G. Rice to answer any telegrams that arrived for me. He received the following:

PETERSBURG, ILL., May 7, 1885.
To HENRY CRASKE, Rushville, Ill.:
Menard gave Weaver two hundred and seven majority. How is Schuyler? Answer. S. H. BLANE.

The following reply was sent:

RUSHVILLE, ILL., May 7, 1885.
To S. H. BLANE, Petersburg, Ill.:
Schuyler gives Weaver probably one hundred or more.
HENRY CRASKE.

On Friday morning, the 8th, I received the following message from Gen. Logan:

SPRINGFIELD, ILL., May 7, 1885.
To HENRY CRASKE, Rushville, Ill.:
Look closely after returns and certificate. Democratic programme is to delay count.
JOHN A. LOGAN.

I immediately called upon County Clerk Bogue and asked him if he had forwarded abstract of returns to Springfield. He informed me he had sent them out on the early mail. I told him I was very glad of that as an effort was being made to delay returns.

The following message was immediately sent to Gen. Logan:

RUSHVILLE, ILL., May 8, 1885.

To Hon. JOHN A. LOGAN, Springfield, Ill.:

Abstract mailed at eight thirty this morning. Official, one hundred and sixty-one for Weaver. Send us official from other counties. We are very anxious.

HENRY CRASKE.

About 1 o'clock, P. M., County Clerk Bogue came to me and said: "Harry, what did you mean when you were asking those questions this morning?" I then showed him Gen. Logan's message. He appeared to be very angry, and said: "I have just received this dispatch from Virginia," and handed it to me, saying, "I wonder what that fellow takes me for. As an official, I know no party. As a private citizen, of course, I would do anything that is honorable to defeat the Republican party." Mr. Bogue gave me permission to wire a copy of the dispatch to Gen. Logan. He also expressed a desire that it should be done, "For," said he, "I do not want those gentlemen at Springfield to think, for a moment, that I would lend myself to the purpose of holding back the returns; especially as I sent word some time before the election to the supervisors of the townships to forward returns as soon as counted, so I could send official returns to Springfield, Friday. Of course, the election has resulted different from what was expected; but that does not alter my duty."

I then wired the following:

RUSHVILLE, ILL., May 8, 1885.

To HON. JOHN A. LOGAN, Springfield, Ill.:

Telegram just received by county clerk, who requested me to wire you the facts. Telegram reads: "Hold back returns seven days. [Signed] *—, —, ———

Virginia, Cass county."

Schuyler is safe.

HENRY CRASKE.

——*The name is withheld by request. It was sent to Gen. Logan.

The name signed was that of a prominent county official of Cass county. The name is withheld now at the request of Mr. Bogue.

About 6 o'clock, P. M., the following dispatch was received from Gen. Logan:

SPRINGFIELD, ILL., May 8, 1885.

To H. CRASKE, Rushville, Ill.:

Dispatch received. Menard 206 majority for Weaver, Cass 93 for Leeper, Mason 20 for Weaver. This is about correct. Thanks to your clerk for doing his duty.

JOHN A. LOGAN.

CHAPTER V.

OFFICIAL RETURNS.

CASS COUNTY.

The following is the official vote of Cass county; also the official vote for Presidential Electors, in 1884:

	Arthur A. Leeper.	W. H. Weaver.	Cleveland.	Blaine.
Ashland	103	125	177	105
Arenzville	66	45	176	140
Beardstown	274	354	519	464
Bluff Springs ...	21	20	84	70
Oregon	36	33	117	71
Chandlerville ...	114	57	176	87
Hickory	8	2	49	35
Indian Creek	11	...	55	20
Monroe	21	19	70	24
Princeton.......	12	26	100	59
Philadelphia	35	32	47	42
Richmond	87	26	135	48
Virginia	220	177	351	240
Total	1008	916	2056	1 405
Majority	92		651	

MENARD COUNTY.

The following is the official vote of Menard county; also the official vote for Presidential Electors, in 1884:

	Arthur A. Leeper.	W. H. Weaver.	Cleveland.	Blaine.
Athens.	47	181	182	262
Greenview	63	77	137	178
Indian Creek....	53	46	104	63
Petersburg, poll 1	135	109	349	153
Petersburg, poll 2	103	70	223	121
Rock Creek.....	6	46	133	68
Sand Ridge.....	11	....	241	58
Sweetwater	38	83	85	99
Tallula	32	88	125	132
Total	488	700	1579	1134
Majority....		212	445	

MASON COUNTY.

The following is the official vote of Mason county, also the official vote for Presidential Electors, in 1884:

	Arthur A. Leeper.	W. H. Weaver.	Cleveland.	Blaine.
Allens Grove....	31	77	129	117
Bath	67	40	211	93
Crane Creek	19	21	111	60
Forest City	32	54	103	86
Havana..........	308	179	471	329
Kilbourne	28	40	96	73
Lynchburg......	30	29	79	50
Manito	40	19	140	100
Mason City	158	231	293*	269
Pennsylvania ...	10	32	79	60
Quiver	17	43	74	93
Salt Creek	34	75	99	96
Sherman........	19	8	113	59
Total	793	848	2016	1485
Majority		55	531	

SCHUYLER COUNTY.

The following is the official vote of Schuyler county; also the official vote for Presidential Electors, in 1884:

	Arthur A. Leeper.	W. H. Weaver.	Cleveland.	Blaine.
Oakland	164	50	144	99
Littleton........	64	114	101	140
Brooklyn.......	29	65	100	145
Birmingham	27	123	78	148
Huntsville	60	69	126	101
Camden	61	30	168	73
Buenavista......	103	120	211	168
Rushville.......	197	205	319	290
Browning.......	115	69	215	92
Hickory.........	25	15	82	28
Frederick	11	47	47	56
Bainbridge	60	66	177	108
Woodstock	91	47	188	85
Total.	859	1020	1956	1533
Majority....		161	423	

CHAPTER VI.

SELECTING THE CANDIDATE.

On **Tuesday** evening, April 28th, the following gentlemen **met at** Gen. Logan's room at the Leland Hotel: . **Gen.** Logan, Daniel Shepard, Sam. Jones, **Jake Wheeler,** Reuben Lancaster, Charles **B.** Gatton, James B. Black, and Perry Logsdon. At this meeting, the plan forwarded to Gen. Logan on April 16th was presented by him, discussed and approved, and Thursday was the day agreed upon as the time to select a candidate. Daniel Shepard invited the following gentlemen to be present at Thursday's meeting: Gen. Lippincott and Tree **Mathews,** of Cass; Wells Corey, of Mason; Col. Judy and Capt. **S. H.** Blane, of Menard. Of those invited, Capt. **S. H.** Blane, and Wells Corey responded in person. There were **also** present Gen. Logan, Daniel Shepard, secretary of Republican State Central Committee, Jacob Wheeler of Internal Revenue Department, and **Hon.** Samuel Jones of Springfield, Reuben Lancaster and Dr. S. Colladay of Virginia, Cass **county.** This meeting was held in the room occupied **by** Hon. Wm. R. Morrison **until** a few **days** before, when he had **given it up and** started for Washington. The *coterie* of gentlemen **who** assembled **on** this occasion were anything but favorable to Morrison's election to the **U. S.** Senate.

Of **the names presented, that of** John **T.** Beekman **was** selected as the **most available.** Persons from

Cass county objected to him on account of his being in favor of low license; but this objection was not considered at this meeting. Weaver's name was also suggested, but no action taken. After the meeting was over, it was decided that, on account of their failure to agree on Beekman, it should be left to the gentlemen from Menard county to make the nomination.

Wells Corey was empowered to print tickets. (The tickets cost Gen. Logan fifteen dollars; and this was all the election expenses that were defrayed by persons at Springfield. It should be remembered that there was no money used in this campaign excepting what was absolutely necessary, such as horse-and-buggy-hire, and feed for horses, board and lodging for men, while attending to the work. This expense was paid by the gentlemen who had charge of the work in their respective counties.)

Capt. S. H. Blane agreed to send the name of the candidate, as soon as one should be selected, to Mr. Corey at Mason City, so that tickets could be printed without delay. Upon arrival at Petersburg, Capt. Blane called a caucus. Capt. W. H. Weaver being the choice of the caucus, he was interviewed at once, and finally consented to permit his name to be used. Mr. Corey was duly notified of the fact. He printed tickets and sent them to the several distributing points, namely: Havana, Petersburg, Virginia, and Rushville.

Maj. Ruggles of Havana, Theodore Bell of Quiver Township, and Wells Corey of Mason City, are the gentlemen who finally had the management of affairs in Mason county.

CHAPTER VII.

JOURNEY TO THE CAPITAL.

On Monday, May 11th, W. I. Larash and the author drove to Frederick, whence we went by rail to Springfield, where we arrived in company with Hon. Perry Logsdon, about 5 o'clock, P. M. Soon after our arrival, we met Hon. Jacob Wheeler, who invited us to go to the Leland Hotel with him to see Gen. Logan; but, Mr. Logsdon having a prior engagement elsewhere, our visit to the General was deferred until later in the day. About 9 o'clock, in the evening, we met Gen. Logan at the Leland. After introductions, the General exclaimed: "My God! boys, I did n't believe it practicable; I have known of similar work being done in a town, or in a connty, but in a district composed of four counties, I did not believe it could be done. I pronounce it the most daring piece of political strategy, so successfully executed, since the days of Alexander the Great."

In the meantime, the Democrats were doing all they could to pick flaws in the returns from some of the precincts in Mason, Menard, and Cass counties, and had sent a great many statesmen from the capital to look after matters a little, you know. Presumably to encourage the clerks to hold back the official returns, the full seven days allowed by law. The time wore away, however, and official returns finally reached Springfield. Those of Mason and Menard came by the Thursday morning (May 14th) mail. The Cass county returns were in charge of a special messenger who was patiently awaited all day. On the arrival of the 4:30 train from Beardstown, a special conveyance, with Manning Logan in charge, was in waiting at the depot. The messenger entered it and was immediately driven to the State House, where the State Canvassers met and the official canvass was concluded and the Governor's signature attached to the Weaver certificate at 5:10, P. M. The House, however, had adjourned till 10 o'clock, Friday morning, and the Representatives were obliged to wait to make their new accession available.

When the joint assembly met, pursuant to adjournment, at 7:30, P. M., and Weaver's certificate having been issued in the meantime, the Republicans determined to have the oath of office administered and ask to have him seated, so that he could take part in the joint session; but, by some means the plan miscarried. The joint assembly adjourned till Friday, 8:30, A. M. Immediately after the adjournment of the evening joint session, however, Mr. Weaver took his certificate to Judge Gross, who was on the floor of the House and demanded that he administer the oath of office to him. Judge Gross administered the oath.

On Friday morning, after a hard fight, the Democrats, when they found they could not help themselves, finally agreed to allow Capt. W. H. Weaver to take his seat; provided, the Republicans would agree to cast only formal ballots until Tuesday, the

19th, when **real balloting was to be the order** of the day.

Tuesday at length arrived, and on the first ballot Gen. Logan was elected, after a long delay caused by the filibustering tactics of the Democrats, who were willing to vote for any one **or** anything to beat Logan. But the gallant 103 Republicans stood firm and undaunted through the trying ordeal.

On motion of Representative Fuller, the Chair appointed Messrs. Fuller, Chapman and Merritt, a committee **of three** to conduct General Logan into **the hall.** When Logan appeared, walking down the aisle on the arm of Senator Merritt, **a** scene **of the** wildest enthusiasm ensued and it was some minutes before he **could be** heard. He was introduced by **Speaker Haines and** spoke as follows:

"*Gentlemen of the Senate and House of Representatives of the State of Illinois:*

"I congratulate you on having brought to a conclusion this most remarkable contest, which has been going **on** for nearly four months. I **have** no words **to** express my gratitude to the representatives **of this** great State of Illinois for the compliment they have **paid** me to-day. Having been elected for the third time to represent this great State in the Senate **of the United** States, I hope I have so acted and deported myself, my party, **my** State and country; and my past history is the only guarantee I can give for my future course. From the **deepest** recess of **my** bosom, I again thank you for the honor you **have conferred upon** me. There is no position on earth **which could** be more gratifying than to represent this **great State. In this** contest, which has been **an unusually close and heated one,** I am proud to state that nothing has transpired **to mar the** friendly relations existing between myself **and** my worthy opponent. For thirty years, this gentleman and **my** self have been friends, and I trust we shall always remain such. [Loud cheers.] I believe there has never **been** a contest between two persons waged more **earnestly for** their parties than this, after which the mutual relations of the candidates remained so pleasant. I respect Mr. Morrison politically and socially, and am proud to say we are friends, and sincerely hope we may ever be friends. [Cheers.] As to the other gentleman who was my opponent for a time, I can say nothing against him, nor would I want to. Mr. Tree and myself lived neighbors for many years in Chicago, and I have always had the highest respect for him. He made as good a contest, coming late into the field and being a little short of votes, as he could make. For him, I have nothing but respect. In conclusion, gentlemen, I desire to say that, no matter what may have occurred during this contest, it has been carried on in a spirit of fairness. No such contest has ever been known in this country before, and it has appeared strange to me that there has been so little bitterness and excitement exhibited. It is remarkable, I say, in a contest which has lasted so long and been so close, that there is so little bitterness of feeling displayed, and I desire to say that, in representing the people of this State of Illinois in the United States Senate, I shall ever try to do that which seems to me to be my duty—representing my party and my constituents fairly and honestly. [Cheers.] I leave here having no bitter feeling towards any one who may have opposed me. I respect a man who will stand by his creed and his friends, and I expect no more from others accorded to me. If I go to Washington, I do not go there with any fire burning in my bosom, or feeling of antagonism toward any party or the present Administration. I shall endeavor to represent you fairly and honestly, and stand by you in all which I believe to be right. Gentlemen, again I thank you—I tender you my most profound thanks. I have not before repaid, nor can I repay, you for the manner in which you have stood by me in this Legislature and State. I shall ever remember it, and endeavor to prove worthy of the trust this day confided in me. Thanking you again, I hope you will learn in the future that the wrong man has not been elected." [Applause and cheers.]

The Hon. Perry Logsdon and W. I. Larash called at the headquarters of Gen. Logan on the afternoon of May 20th, and before taking their leave,

the General requested Mr. Larash to be the bearer
of the following letter addressed to the author:

LELAND HOTEL, SPRINGFIELD, ILL., May 20th, 1885.

HENRY CRASKE—*My Dear Sir:* The election is over and the
victory is ours. To the Thirty-Fourth Representative District are
we indebted for the vote that gave us the majority in the Legislature, and to you, my dear sir, there is much due for the organization and success. You were the first man who suggested to me
the possibility of carrying the district. I wrote you then, saying
the plan was a good one. Of course great credit is due to all our
friends who aided in carrying out the program, from whom I
would not wish to detract anything, but to you I give the credit
as the originator of the plan which was a success, and to you I
now return my grateful acknowledgements.

Your Friend,

[Signed]   JOHN A. LOGAN.

[See facsimile on opposite page.]

LELAND HOTEL

Springfield, Ill., May 20, 1893

Henry Cursold,

My dear Sir

The election is over and the victory is ours. To the 34th Miss. Bill, we are now indebted for the vote that gave us the majority in the Legislature, and to you my dear Sir, this is largely due for the organization was done. You were the first man who suggested to me the possibility of carrying the district. I wrote you then saying the plan was a good one, of course great credit is due to all our friends who aided in carrying out the programme, from whom I would not wish to abstract anything, but to you I give the credit as the originator of the plan which was a success, and to you I must return my grateful acknowledgments.

Your friend

John A. Draper

CHAPTER VIII.

PREVALENCE OF THE INSPIRATION.

It will be seen by the following letters and items that the idea of electing a Republican was quite prevalent among the active Republican workers of the district:

The following letter was received on April 20th, by Jacob Hammond, postmaster at Rushville, from John Waner, of Birmingham, Schuyler county:

April 19, 1883.

JACOB HAMMOND, Rushville, Ill.:

Dear Sir: As everything is Democratic, have we not got a good chance to elect a Republican in place of Mr. Shaw (deceased), to the House of Representatives and make Logan, U. S. Senator? I have been thinking that we could defeat the Democratic nominee if every working Republican in the district was posted, and would work on the sly, and get every Republican out on the afternoon of May 6th, we could defeat the Democratic nominee.

I haven't talked to any person yet, and will not until I hear from you. You don't want more than two or three in each township to know anything about it, and let them be the right kind and I know it will work. I think anything, except stealing or murder, would be honorable to do to elect a Republican, if that would elect J. A. Logan senator.

I may be a little "off", in your estimation, but I would as soon see Jeff. Davis elected as to see Logan defeated. Jeff. Davis may die, and I want Logan there, when the "Rebels" disgrace the flag by lowering at half-mast to honor a d—d rebel; as they did for that traitor, Thompson. My language is not sufficient to do the subject justice. Yours, JOHN WANER.

W. W. Potts, of Rushville, in a conversation with Maj. B. C. Gillam, suggested the possibility of carrying the district, and asked the Major to see the author in regard to the matter. Maj. Gillam approached me on Thursday, April 23d, and said: "Harry, can't we do something to carry this district?" He was told that something was being done and was cautioned to keep still.

In Mason county, Mr. Theodore Bell considered the matter seriously. He wrote the following letter to Hon. Jacob Wheeler:

TOPEKA, ILL., April 25, 1885.

FRIEND JAKE: I believe, with the proper amount of systematic work all over the district, we can elect a Republican on the 6th of May. My plan is to have the Republicans come to the polls to vote late in the day, so that the Democrats can't rally on us. This can be done by having a good trusty Republican in every neighborhood to notify the Republicans and bring them to the polls. These are busy times with the farmers, and they won't come to vote unless urged to come; and there has been very little said about the election and hundreds of voters in the district do n't know on what day the election is called. The Democrats will be napping, and if we are wide-awake we will "get there."

Write me what you think of this. I would work this up all over the district if I had the money to spend, but I have not.

Very truly yours,

THEO. BELL.

It will be seen from the foregoing that this spirit was agitating some of the Republicans all over the district. In Virginia, Cass county, on Monday evening, April 27th, the following gentlemen met at Dr. S. Colladay's office, namely: Dr. Colladay, Reuben Lancaster, Charles B. Gatton, and James B. Black. The question was raised as to the feasibility of carrying the district for the Republican party. It was determined that Mr. Black, Mr. Lancaster, and Mr. Gatton should go to Springfield next day, the 28th, for the purpose of interviewing Hon. Perry Logsdon on the subject. This explains the presence of these gentlemen at the meeting in Gen. Logan's room, on the evening of April 28th.

It has been the aim of the author to place upon the Roll of Honor the name of every Republican who was engaged in the work, and to give each one the full measure of praise that is justly due him. If any one is omitted, it is the fault of memory and not the intentional ommission of the author.

CHAPTER IX.

CAMPAIGN IN CASS COUNTY.

The following is a letter received from Hon. F. M. Davis in regard to the campaign in the Beardstown precinct:

BEARDSTOWN, ILL., July 15, 1885.

HENRY CRASKE, Rushville, Ill.:

DEAR SIR: At your request, I send you the particulars of the election held at Beardstown, on May 6th, 1885, for Representative to the Legislature from the Thirty-Fourth District.

I would state that the first information I received in the matter was a visit to my home by yourself and Col. Asa C. Matthews, on the Sunday preceding the election. So short was your visit that no one suspected the mission you were on. Upon your information that John T. Beekman was our candidate, and to carry out the instructions of the circular you gave me, I went to work immediately. On Monday evening, Wm. H. Weaver was the candidate. On Tuesday evening, a meeting was called at T. K. Condit's house, and the following persons were present: T. L. Mathews, T. K. Condit, Alex. Forsyth, C. Pilger, and F. M. Davis, of Beardstown, and Charles Condit, of Arenzville. After talking the matter over, it was agreed that I should attend to the distribution of the tickets, exercising the greatest care that none but staunch Republicans receive the tickets. Instructions were also given that none should go near the polls sooner than 4 o'clock, P. M., which progamme was carried out to the letter, with the exception of a few Republicans who came from the country.

At 12, M., only twenty-seven votes had been cast. At 1 o'clock, the Democrats at Ashland telephoned to the Democratic Committee here that tickets had been found bearing the name of W. H. Weaver; but that no such tickets had been voted, so far. The Democratic Committee replied that it would not amount to anything; that no one was voting here; that only forty votes were polled, and there was no use to give it any attention, as Leeper was sure of election.

I gave tickets to several Republicans who could keep a secret, to be given to Republicans who were working around at different places in the city; and by 4 o'clock, there was more winking, as one Republican would meet another, than I ever saw. Mr. Alex. Forsyth and W. C. Brown were appointed to supply the railroad men with tickets, and they performed this duty well. C. Pilger's duty was to watch the voters from the country and send them back to the country precincts, which duty he performed acceptably, by sending home on the double-quick, some of the voters who voted at Bluff Springs precinct. The vote out there (only one majority for Leeper) tells the story.

Up to 4 o'clock, the Democrats had not found out that we had a candidate in the person of W. H. Weaver. At that time, they were convinced that something was up, and they went to work with all their might. But so still had the Republicans kept their secret, that the die was irrevocably cast. Several Democrats were told at this time, and Weaver tickets handed them, which they voted, on being told that his election would elect John A. Logan to the U. S. Senate.

. This precinct, which in November gave Cleveland Electors sixty-six majority, gave Weaver a majority of eighty. The official vote is as follows: Weaver, 354; Leeper, 274; total, 628.

Some of the Democrats were very angry on receipt of news of Weaver's election; but a great many were glad, and so expressed themselves; saying that Logan was the choice of the people of the whole State and ought to be elected, as he was such a brave general and grand statesman.

Yours, respectfully,   F. M. DAVIS.

ASHLAND, ILL., July 14th, 1885.

H. CRASKE.—*Dear Sir:* By your request I will give a few details, or happenings, of the election here on May 6th, 1885, in this noted district, the Thirty-Fourth, in regard to the Weaver *vs.* Leeper campaign for Representative.

On Monday before the election, I went to Havana (by way of Virginia) to visit my sister who was at the time dangerously sick. While I was waiting for my train at Virginia, I was informed of the plan by Reuben Lancaster, of that place. He wanted me to take the tickets and come back and work our precinct. As I was obliged to go to Havana, I prevailed on him to go to Ashland that night, and place the tickets in the hands of Wm. S. Douglas.

While I was still in Virginia, I met the Democratic candidate for Representative. The first words he spoke was to accuse me of working some scheme to defeat him; and after I had gone to the depot, he and his friend, Jack McDonald, came there to interview me. I assured them that if I was working such a scheme I would endeavor not to "give it away." I jokingly retorted that it would be a nice thing for the Republican party if such a thing could be done. As the train was late and they were still uneasy, they concluded to go to Havana with me and see what I was going to do. As we passed through Snicarte, a place consisting of only two or three houses and a few corn cribs and is almost lost in a desert of sand, Jack McDonald (the friend of the Democratic candidate) remarked to me that he thought that would be a good place for my candidate to come to the next day after the election. He seemed to think that Snicarte was a very lonely place and a good place for a defeated candidate. I have never heard whether Leeper ever went there or not. After reaching Havana, the first man I found was Lawyer Brown. I informed him of their business and put him on their track to throw them off, if possible. This he (Brown) did completely, and they returned to Virginia the next morning, feeling assured the coast was clear.

I returned home to Ashland the next morning, and found Wm. Douglas in the height of his glory; and that afternoon, his son Charles was exhibiting a fine stallion all over the precinct. He was a Republican horse and, of course, was only shown to the Republicans, as everybody knows a Democrat would not have anything to do with a Republican horse. Several of us had business in the country at that time, but all in different directions, and no suspicion was created to alarm Democrats.

All went lovely until about **10** o'clock on the day of the election, when they received a telegram to look out,—that the Republicans were going to spring a candidate; but we baffled them by abusing the saloons, threatening to prosecute them for keeping open doors on election day. We protested that saloons had to be closed on *all* election days. While we were parleying over that, they forgot all about the election until **1** o'clock, when another telegram came stating that there was surely a Republican candidate out, and that they must go to work at once; but they could not believe it as there had been only three Republican votes during the day. They, however, got to pushing us too hard and we saw we had to get up some excitement to keep them quiet, so we commenced on this little scheme: There was an old foundation of a wind-mill which had about five feet of water in it, and the little boys were fishing almost continually there. The project was to take a baby's dress and cut a few holes in it with a knife and sprinkle it with blood, and have some good-sized boy fish it out, and pretend he saw the dead body in the water. It was all done in less time than I have been writing this. It was a grand success. In less than a half-hour there were two or three hundred people crowding around the old foundation, expecting every minute to see some one rake up the dead and murdered baby. Even the judges of the election had to take their turns and visit the place of search. One very amusing thing was, every Republican believed there was a baby there. After failing to find it with rakes, some one proposed to dip the water out, so as to be sure; and in about twenty minutes there were nearly a hundred buckets in operation pailing out the water. There being two or three hundred barrels of water to pail out, it continued until about 4 o'clock, when some Republican, carelessly, "gave it away," and now the ball commenced rolling. Some of the Democrats could not believe there was anything of it. Others believed it, but had no fears of a defeat and bragged how easily they "caught on" and expressed themselves as believing that they would have been defeated if they had not found it out.

At 4 o'clock, there were over ninety votes polled and only three for Weaver. At 6 o'clock, when the votes were counted, Weaver was twenty-two votes ahead. As this precinct went thirty-six Democratic last fall, this made the Democrats feel pretty blue. We soon heard, by telegraph, that Greenview had given Weaver a majority of eighty. Next came Athens, one hundred and seventy-four majority for Weaver. Beardstown, seventy-six for Weaver.

A Democrat was not now to be found and the town was full of Republicans. Anvils were being fired, flags were floating in the breeze, and excitement was unbounded. Every message that came was so much for Weaver, and thus it continued. A great many of us kept up the enthusiasm until John A. Logan was re-elected U. S. Senator. This was our purpose all the time; and not until then did we get satisfaction. The Democrats have not fully recovered yet. Whether they ever will or not is to be seen in the future. It is to be hoped that they never will.

Hoping this will be of some benefit to you and that we may win for our "Black Jack" what he richly deserves, the presidency in 1888,

I am yours, truly,   A. F. BURNHAM, M.D.

CHAPTER X.

CAMPAIGN IN MENARD COUNTY.

The following is a brief history of the "still hunt" in Menard county, as furnished me by a prominent Republican of Petersburg:

PETERSBURG, ILL., July 16, 1885.

HENRY CRASKE, Esq.:—*Dear Sir.* Enclosed find brief sketch of campaign here: The history of the "still hunt" in Menard county may be briefly told. On April 29th, a letter was received by Capt. S. H. Blane, from Henry Craske, of Rushville, Schuyler county, submitting the plan which was afterward substantially adopted and carried out. In the Craske letter was also one from R. W. Mills, of Virginia, Cass county, approving the scheme and nominating Capt. Blane for Representative. By same mail, a communication was received from Dan. Shepard, written at Springfield, requesting an interview at the Leland, on the 30th. On the day last named, room 14 at the Leland found several gentlemen assembled, whose conversation was not very loud. Captain Blane declined to run and urged his ineligibility by reason of holding the office of State's Attorney in his county. It was thought best by those present that Menard county should furnish the candidate. Several names were discussed, among others that of John T. Beekman, and it was finally agreed that he should be the candidate; but objections were raised by some gentlemen from one of the other counties and it was afterward agreed that another should be selected. It was left for Menard county to select and report name to Wells Corey, of Mason City, who had agreed to print the tickets and send them by express to the different counties.

On the way home on the train, Mr. Corey and Capt. Blane continued the question of candidate. Mr. Corey spoke favorably of Capt. Weaver on account of his extensive acquaintance in three of the counties. Arriving at Petersburg by the evening train after the shades of night had fallen, the telephone was called into requisition and by a sort of "cipher-alley" conversation a small *coterie* of Republicans were soon in consultation. Three names were prominently before the conspirators. Capt. Weaver's was first on the list. He was to be seen, urged to run, and, in case of his refusal, then the second was to be seen; and, in case of his refusal, the third was to be called on. A committee of two called at Capt. W. H. Weaver's residence and were invited in, the Captain being in another room. Upon recognizing the voices of the two callers, he came in, *sans* coat and vest, *sans* boots, *sans* shirt collar, and smilingly apologized for the situation, and invited his friends to be seated. Drawing their chairs up close to the Captain, one on each side, the night prowlers opened on their unsuspecting victim. The political situation was broached, Gen. Logan's chances discussed, his sacrifice in the late presidential election referred to, and about the time Capt. Weaver's blood began to warm up at the recollection of St. John's villainy, and Dr. Burchard's infirmity, the subject-matter of the visit was introduced. The Captain was taken unawares. He pleaded poverty,—he was too poor to make the race, and could not afford to drop his business and incur the necessary expense of the race.

These objections were promptly met by the personal assurance that the campaign should not cost him a dollar. He urged the names of other Republicans. Each name was objected to, when compared with his own, as not the best, all things considered. The great importance of the situation was urged upon him; the far-reaching effects of success, if obtained; the great consolation there would come from snatching victory from the jaws of defeat; and how much of the poison of last fall's humiliation would be extracted if Gen. Logan was sent back to the U. S. Senate. The Captain fully entered into the spirit of these matters, and finally said, if the two friends who were urging his candidacy, really considered it a duty to the Republican party and Gen. Logan for him to run, he would consent to lead the forlorn hope, and take the consequences, for better or for worse.

In five minutes, the "still hunt" began. A few of the faithful were let into the secret, but "mum's the word." The most of the actual canvassing was done the two days and nights previous to the election. The tickets were printed by that prince of Republicans, Wells Corey, and by him sent to the several distributing points. Tickets were sent out by private messengers to the proper men in each precinct, with instructions that no other word by mail or otherwise would be sent; but each man was to work up his own precinct, without asking further questions. To get the tickets and word to the several precincts without creating suspicion was the most difficult part of the campaign. John Purkapile, a wounded soldier, who of late years had been buying butchers' stock for the Petersburg butchers, was called in, given the "countersign" and directed to be ready on a certain morning to proceed to certain points in the east part of the county. The morning designated found Purkapile on his blue-roan pony, with a cattle-whip coiled around the horn of his saddle, and with a couple of shepherd dogs following. He started on his journey, making frequent inquiries for "butchers' stock," of all Democratic travelers he met on the road. It is estimated that the number of beeves looked at on that trip and conditionally bargained for would fill a respectable army contract. According to instructions, Purkapile rounded up about noon at "Bob" Young's, near Indian Point. "Bob,'" by the way, is an old soldier and had been in Petersburg a day or so previously, and when Purkapile rode up it was somewhat surprising to "Bob's" family that he, obviously, had been expecting a visitor. After dinner, Purkapile meandered on eastward to the residence of Henry C. Graham, where another order was delivered, and from there to E. C. Read's, in the Sweetwater precinct, Purkapile and his shepherd dogs wended their way intent on bringing in a herd of fat cows, if any could be bought "right,"—this being very difficult to do that day.

John Willson, an insurance agent, was sent out into other parts of the county to deliver tickets. It was somewhat remarkable to the Democrats how quickly this insurance agent would get through talking insurance.

One Republican, Eli Reep, in the west part of the county, had a great deal of trouble, apparently, in finding the kind of seed corn he wanted. For two days and nights prior to the election, he was riding about the country, sampling everyone's seed-corn, and declaring he was greatly discouraged at the unsoundness of the "sprout." As he has made no complaint lately, we presume he found some that grew.

Saul Austill, an old war-horse of the "sixties," at Sweetwater, found his health a "little off" for a couple of days before the election, and loitered around the postoffice, where he met a great many men from the country. He apparently wanted to buy a work-horse; as he followed a number of farmers to their wagons and was examining their horses' limbs and occasionally got in and drove the team around a little.

In the Greenview precinct, "Bob" Killion kept the boys quiet and in line until the pre-arranged hour of 5 o'clock, when they were turned loose to the great consternation of the "unterrified." It was afterward remarked by some of the observing Democrats, who can see better out of their hindsights than they can out of their foresights, that Homer Tice had to salt his cattle in a distant pasture several times the last few days before the election.

In the Tallula district, John T. Beekman, George C. Spears, "Dock" Glenn, John Q. Spears, C. C. Judy, and John Haley Spears moved on the enemy in splendid style. Dr. Robertson, an old-time Bourbon, remarked frequently during election day, that it seemed to him the Republicans were just completely whipped out, as they did not have enough spunk left to even bring out a candidate. To these remarks, the boys returned very vague answers, telling the old doctor that, since Cleveland had been elected, they had concluded to "let the tail go with the hide." When the time came and the Republicans began to vote, the old doctor remarked that they ought to have brought out their man sooner and let him receive a respectable vote. The next morning he concluded the "respectable vote" was lacking for the other man.

In the Petersburg precinct, the strictest secrecy was observed. But few knew anything of the scheme. Men, usually active in political affairs, were ignorant of what was going on; and, when the Democrats became somewhat suspicious, they naturally plied these old-time politicians with questions, watched their movements, and neither hearing nor seeing anything about them out of the usual routine, settled down complacently in the assurance that all was right. The secret conspirators were sorely tried to keep a careless and indifferent exterior, and in passing each other on the street adopted Burns' idea to "look as ye were na lookin' at me." Secret caucuses were held late at night in the third story of a certain furniture store, where, by the dim light of a turn-down lamp, showed the queer surroundings, where "coffins stood 'round like open presses," which, while they did not show the "dead in their last dresses," suggested to the caucus the possibility of a corpse being in preparation to occupy one of them in the very near future. The manner in which this upper story was reached without arousing suspicion, the way each fellow would "syne up the back stile, and let nae body see," can better be imagined than described. The many hair-breadth escapes from discovery were too numerous to relate. Secrecy had to be enforced, and yet the Republican voters had to be notified.

One instance will illustrate the manner of getting out the Petersburg vote. Ed. Goodman, a plasterer, whitewasher, and brick-mason, took his whitewash bucket on his arm the morning of the election, and with pole and brush on his shoulder started out through the resident part of town apparently looking for a job. When he called at a Republican's house he, of course, made his business known secretly and passed. Did he meet a Democrat, his inquiry was for a job, which, if ready for him would be declined under some pretext, until some future day.

There was little talk on the streets or in public places. It is impossible to give the names of all who actively worked out the scheme. There was one watch-word which never failed to enlist the most lethargic Republican,—the name of John A. Logan. When the plan was revealed to a "doubting Thomas," the assurance that Logan was personally interested and was expecting every Republican to do his duty, was sufficient to put him to work. The potency of Logan's name was remarkable. Its mention set on fire the latent enthusiasm of every man to whom the subject was introduced.

In Athens precinct, Henry C. Graham, "Bob" Young, "Buck" Williams, Capt. Hurt, W. S. Hurt, Jeff. Johnson, John Kinhart, J. H. Kincaid, John A. Kincaid, R. Y. Kincaid, and many others managed the campaign skillfully.

The names of Petersburg workers are too numerous to mention. Among them were the following: C. R. Collin, D. M. Bone, W. R. Park, John Purkapile, Ed. Goodman, George Freeze, Capt. McDougall, John Harper, A. Golden, John Willson, S. H. Blane, N. W. Branson, George Morris, W. T. Beekman, and Capt. Weaver.

It is thought worthy of note that the colored voters in Petersburg were faithful to their convictions. In order to bring them in full force to the polls it was only necessary to tell them John A. Logan needed their votes.   Yours,   ————————.

CHAPTER XI.

ANECDOTES.

A TALLULA DEMOCRAT VOTES FOR WEAVER.

This anecdote comes from Tallula, Menard county, as told by that staunch Republican, G. C. Spears, in answer to a request for the particulars:

TALLULA, ILL., July 27, 1885.

HENRY CRASKE, RUSHVILLE, ILL.—*Dear Sir:* Yours of the 21st received in due time. Should have answered sooner but have been quite sick for the last week, better this morning.

You wished me to write you about my Democratic friend voting the Republican ticket. I have no objection to giving the circumstances, but must withhold the name, as he is very sensitive on that subject.

We were working very quietly and the Democrats not suspecting anything. My friend, W. C. Roe, one of our mischievous Republicans, said, "I am going to make 'Sam' vote for Weaver." Seeing him standing on the opposite side of the street, he (Roe) approached him thus: "Sam, have you voted yet?" "No. There is no use of voting, for there is no opposition, and our man will be elected any way. But I ought to vote, for I went to school to that man." "Well, I think so, too. Come on. I will go with you and vote," giving him a ticket (a Weaver ticket folded up), so they walked to the polls, "Sam" voting first, then Roe. After voting, he saw some Weaver tickets. "What does this mean? Is Weaver running?" Roe replied, "Of course, he is; and you voted for him.' He exclaimed, "That beats the d—l!"

I can join you a hearty hurrah for John A. Logan for the next president.

Respectfully,　　G. C. SPEARS.

CAPT. WEAVER'S STORY.

There is a story extant that is very amusing in regard to an aged Republican of Mason county, who went to Havana early on the morning of May 6th. Upon inquiry, he was assured by the Democrats that Mr. Leeper was the only candidate running, and they insisted that he must vote for him. He, however, declined to do so; but they continued to insist, and, using some of their persuasive methods, finally induced him to vote for Leeper. The old Republican started for home about 5 o'clock, P. M. On the road, he met a number of Republican neighbors who informed him they were going to town to vote. He told them it was no use, as they would have to vote for Leeper, as he was the only candidate that was running.' The neighbors told him he was mistaken; for W. H. Weaver was running, and they were going in to vote for him. The aged Republican now got very angry at himself for being gulled so easily, and induced to vote for the Democratic candidate. He went home loathing himself, and determined to have revenge. He got a rope from the barn and went to the orchard and putting the rope around his neck, threw the end over a limb of the tree, laid hold of it with both hands and drew it tight, then eased up and yelled out, "Vote the Democratic ticket will you? g—d d.—m you." He would then tighten the rope, ease up, and draw himself again until the flesh weakened and he finally took a solemn oath, that if the good Lord would forgive him this time for voting the Democratic ticket, he would never do so any more.

A DESERVED TRIBUTE.

To the Republicans of the Thirty-Fourth Senatorial District, the author wishes to say, that to you, all honor is due for the high state of discipline, organization, and obedience, without which success would not have been possible. To you, therefore, the thanks of the Republicans of the Nation are due. For by your prompt action on the 6th, the grand result desired and hoped for was successfully accomplished on the 19th day of May,—the election of Hon. John A. Logan to the United States Senate. And through you has been demonstrated the fact that thorough disciplined organization and obedience are the necessary adjuncts to a successful political campaign under difficulties. You have also demonstrated the fact that the Republicans can do, and ever have done their most efficient work without hope of pecuniary reward or official position.

NOTE.—Does not this campaign show conclusively that in accomplishing results, good generalship and practical politics are far superior to that peculiar kind known as "sentimental politics" which exists, to some extent, in the Republican party? Are there not Republicans, who, believing in the justice of their cause, think it must be victorious, that if not victorious now, it surely will be by and by, and are thus willing to wait?

To those "goody, goody" fellows allow me to say, that, although we had right and at least 25,000 majority of the voters of the State for the Republican party, General Logan would not have been elected to the U. S. Senate had it not been for that brave and gallant little band of *practical* Republicans, whose good fortune permitted them to live in the Thirty-Fourth Senatorial District of Illinois.

PRESS NOTES.

BEFORE LOGAN'S ELECTION.

The Chicago TIMES, May 8, 1885, says:

The result of the special election in the Thirty-Fourth Legislative District of Illinois is a surprise which is not without decidedly amusing features, though it can hardly be expected that the Democrats will be able to appreciate the comic side of it. The district was admitted to be hopelessly Democratic. In November last every county in it gave a Democratic majority, the aggregate for the district being 2,050. When the vacancy occurred, three or four weeks ago, the majority party nominated a Mr. Leeper to fill it. The Republicans apparently accepted the situation, and, so far as the public knew, had no purpose to contest the election. Mr. Leeper—should not the name have been Sleeper? —and his party certainly accepted the situation—and quite too confidently, as the outcome proves. When election day came, a few Democrats went to the polls in a perfunctory sort of way, and supposed they had elected their man. But suddenly, two or three hours before the closing time, the Republicans began to swarm around the voting places, and, by strict attention to business during the remainder of the day, succeeded in "snowing under" the Democratic ballots in the boxes, and—from the returns at hand at this writing—electing a candidate of their own. The surprise and disgust of Mr. Nye when the "Heathen Chinee" brought out his reserves, in the celebrated contest recorded by Bret Harte, only faintly foreshadowed the feelings of the Thirty-Fourth District Democrats when the trick of their opponents was discovered; for Mr. Nye "went for that Heathen Chinee," and obtained satisfaction and redress, but what balm or solace is there for the abused confidence and bruised feelings of the sufferers from this lost game of ballot-boxing.

A modern proverb asserts that "All's fair in politics," as well as in war. The ambuscade and surprise in the Thirty-Fourth District was certainly as sharp a piece of strategy as has been executed in either field lately; and the Republicans who planned and carried it to success have a right to felicitate themselves upon their shrewdness, the exceeding skill with which they concealed their purpose from the drowsy enemy until the appointed moment, and the energy that brought their forces into the field and won the victory before "night or Blucher" could come to the rescue of the bewildered foe.

Turning from the exultant Republicans, the situation of the Democrats of Illinois, after this unexpected defeat, is found to be most humiliating. Four months ago their legislative representatives assembled at Springfield, exactly equal in numbers to their opponents, but with the prestige of the national victory in November to give them strength and confidence in their ability to elect a United-States Senator. The circumstances and conditions rendered that confidence not unreasonable, and it certainly pervaded the party throughout the State. A caucus selected a candidate, but as soon as the balloting began it became apparent that this chosen standard-bearer was not able to command the full party vote, or to secure the odd man without whom an election was impossible. The opposing candidate was equally unfortunate, some Republicans stubbornly refusing to vote for him; and it was generally admitted that this defection was of a character which would insure the election of any Democrat who could get the votes of all the members chosen as Democrats. From this situation a systematic procrastination and avoidance of plain legal duties was developed by both parties in the legislature. No effort was made by either side to break the "deadlock," or to change the conditions of the contest in any way that might result in breaking it. The captains chosen at the beginning held on to the empty honor of their positions, each seemingly preferring the chance of the other's success in some accidental shuffle of the cards to any action that would leave his party free to seek victory under another leader.

At length a change has come. The death of a Democratic member opened the way for it, and the Republican leaders, by an exploit of almost unparalleled audacity, have elected his sucessor in the face of a vastly superior but feebly commanded host. The senatorial prize, which at almost any time in the last dozen weeks seemed to be within easy reach of a united Democratic force, lies now at the disposal of the Republicans. The responsibility for its loss seems to rest wholly upon the incapable and selfish leaders of the Democrats who, in imbecile inactivity or absorbed in personal ambitions, have permitted themselves and the party to be outgeneraled and outwitted by an alert and energetic foe. The disaster seems to be irremediable. To the party in Illinois and in the country at large, the failure to elect a United-States Senator from this State will appear something in the nature of a calamity; and the mortification and anger with which it must be regarded will be very certain to cause serious discomfort for those to whom it is chargeable.

The Indianapolis (Ind.) JOURNAL, May 18, says:

The duty of the Illinois Legislature is now so palpable, however, and the outcome of its action so important, not only to that but other States, that people not residents of Illinois may be excused for urging prompt and decisive action on this point. Gen. John A. Logan, by his great services in war and his eminent abilities as an active, vigilant member of the United States Senate, has established a reputation as a careful, strong man, peculiarly fitted for the occasion now at hand. In addition to his services as a soldier and legislator, he stands before the Illinois Legislature as the exponent of the National Republican party. He cannot be set aside without harm to the party, and to attempt it or to allow it would be the most stupendous folly. He went into the last National campaign a strong man, and closed it with the prestige of greater popularity than he ever enjoyed. A man who could do what he did is the man for the occasion, and his presence in the Senate is demanded by the Republican party of the entire Nation.

The New York TIMES, May 18:

Gen. John A. Logan should be elected at 12 o'clock to-morrow, or so soon thereafter as the call of the roll can be made.

The Philadelphia PRESS:

If the Republican members of the Illinois Legislature heed the unanimous voice of their party's press, they will elect Gen. Logan at once to the United States Senate. Some of the Independent papers which have heretofore opposed him are also acknowledging his admirable bearing during the long contest and urging his election. It is a good time now, when so many ex-rebels are being placated with office, and loyalty seems to be at a discount, to honor conspicuously a man who remained true to the Government, and who did not fear to declare in the face of Southern threats that "the men of the Northwest will hew their way to the Gulf." There should be no further delay in making this result certain.

The Cleveland LEADER:

Republicans all over the country are united in the opinion that Gen. John A. Logan should now be elected United States Senator from Illinois. The great majority of Democrats also feel that if a Republican is to be elected, it ought to be " Black Jack."

The Chicago MORNING NEWS, May 13:

This is the Republican opportunity. Victory is placed within their grasp through Logan's tenacity of purpose and the political sagacity and adroitness which organized the success in the Thirty-Fourth District.

The Illinois STATE JOURNAL, May 14:

The interest felt in the contest has been National, and has been largely due to the anxiety felt for the re-election of Gen. Logan himself, as well as the desire to see a Republican chosen.

The St. Louis GLOBE-DEMOCRAT, May 16, 1885:

In the whole history of American politics there is scarcely to be found a parallel to the Senatorial contest at Springfield, in the one fact of personal allegiance to a candidate who had neither money nor office to give or to promise as the reward of fidelity. John A. Logan, representing a political party without patronage, and himself a man totally destitute of what the world calls means, has not lost a single supporter out of the even hundred who pledged themselves to him five months ago. They have answered the roll-call every time and are more strongly attached to him to-day than ever before. And yet we are told by some that Logan is a "spoils" politician; that he holds office only by the power of patronage and all that sort of thing. Where are his spoils now? Which one of his supporters can hope for an office in reward for his devotion? To ask the question is to answer it. The spectacle at Springfield on the Republican side is a magnificent one. It is, on one hand, a grand tribute to Logan's worth as a man and as a party leader, and it is, on the other hand, a still grander testimonial to the unselfish devotion of the true men who espoused Logan's payless cause last January, and who will stand by it until it is crowned by success, be it next Tuesday or next Christmas. All honor to Logan and all honor to the Logan men at Springfield.

The NATIONAL TRIBUNE, Washington, D.C., May 21:

Contrary to general expectation nothing was accomplished last week toward electing a Senator from Illinois. The Legislature met in joint session, and Gen. Logan had 103 Republicans present ready to vote for him, but Speaker Haines refused to recognize Weaver because his credentials had not been formally presented. The Democrats made a most astonishing departure, by suddenly dropping their candidates and voting almost solidly for a man named Lambert Tree, of Chicago, whose sole recommendation is that a number of years ago he married a large quantity of Chicago real estate, which has become quite valuable. It is a burning disgrace to the party that it should turn for an instant from such men as Morrison and Black, to attempt to put another mere money-bag in the Senate. There is reason to hope that Gen. Logan will be elected before this paper reaches our readers. Mr. Weaver has presented his credentials in regular form, and has been sworn in. This gives the Republicans a majority of one on joint ballot, and if all are true to their duty— as all promise to be—the election of Gen. Logan is assured.

AFTER LOGAN'S ELECTION.

The St. Louis GLOBE-DEMOCRAT, May 20, 1885:

Grand old Illinois! All honor to the Logan Legion at Springfield. The victorious 103 are worthy successors of the glorious 306. Illinois is a very pronounced Logan State; we said so five months ago. The men who elected John A. Logan to the Senate yesterday paved the way to the triumph of the Republican party in 1888. If the question of Gen. Logan's election to the Senate had been submitted to a vote of the Republicans of the whole country, the result would have been a practically unanimous decision in his **favor**. The **Illinois** Legislature deserves thanks, therefore, for having recognized **the** importance of **doing what is** at once both an advantage to **the State** and a gratification to the party everywhere.

Chicago TRIBUNE, May 20, 1885:

Gen. John A. **Logan** was **yesterday** elected United **States** Senator from Illinois. When the roll was called **it was found** that there were **no absentees in** either house. The announcement that 204 members **of the joint** assembly were present was received with **cheers. When the roll was again** called for Senator, the **Republicans** spoke **one after** another **for** John A. Logan. The Democrats refused to vote. Sittig was silent when his name was reached. The roll-call was finished and 102 votes had been cast for Logan—within one of the **number necessary to elect him.** On **the call** for absentees Sittig **voted** for John A. **Logan,** giving him the necessary **103 votes.** As soon as the enthusiasm which **greeted the** announcement of **Sittig's** vote had subsided **the Dem-** ocrats were permitted to have their say. Their only chance was to try to cause a stampede from Logan to some other Republican; so after voting, most **of** them, for **Tree, they** flew over to Farwell, and **gave** that gentleman **ninety-six votes.** The Republicans, however, stood **solidly** by Gen. Logan, **who** was finally declared **elected.** There was **great** enthusiasm last night all through the **State** over the result **of** the contest, and Senator Logan received letters **from** all **parts of the country** congratulating him **and con-** veying predictions **that he was to be** the next President **of the** United States.

The re-election of John A. **Logan** to the U. S. Senate just as soon as the Republicans secured a majority **of votes on** the joint **ballot** was an event equally honorable to **the successful** candidate and to the Republican members of **the Illinois** Legislature. On Gen. Logan's part, it was a glorious **victory,** earned by a straight- forward, manly, and stubborn fight; **on** the part **of the** Repub- lican members, **it was an evidence that** neither **corruption nor intrigue** could **impair the loyalty of** any man who **had been** elected **as a** Republican. The contest thus closed is **one of the** most remarkable in political records. When the **Legislature met** the two parties were equally divided **on** joint ballot. **Gen. Logan** was the choice **of** the Republican caucus, but personal enmity deprived him of two votes to which he was entitled. Col. Morrison was the nominee of the Demoratic caucus, but was likewise unable to command the full vote of his party. Neither candidate, however, could have been elected as the Legislature was originally constituted, even if he had received all the votes of his party. There was a deadlock which nothing short of treachery and bribery could apparently break. The interests of the rival candidates were watched with the utmost vigilance, and both Democrats and Republicans alternately refrained from voting and thus broke a quorum whenever the other side acquired a temporary advantage. Then death came in as a factor in the fight. First, the Republicans lost a member—Representative Logan of the Nineteenth District. But the Democrats could not summon a quorum in the joint assembly, and there was still no election. A Republican successor to Representative Logan was elected and the tie restored. Then the Democrats lost Senator Bridges of the Thirty-Seventh District, but a Democratic successor was chosen to fill the vacancy caused by his death, and the status remained the same. The turning point came when Representative Shaw, Democrat from the Thirty-Fourth District, died. Here was an opportunity for the Republicans to secure a majority, and, though the district in which the vacancy occurred was Democratic by 2,000 majority, the Logan managers captured it and elected Weaver, a pronounced Logan man.

NATIONAL TRIBUNE, Washington, D. C., May 28, '85: There is a strong satisfaction everywhere at the manner in which the struggle in Illinois has terminated. Gen. Logan's victory is a victory for the old soldiers, whose illustrious representative and champion he is, and it is a victory for the middle classes of the country against the corporations and monopolies, which are threatening to gain complete control of the Senate. Gen. Logan is a poor man, and this is one of his highest claims to honor. He has devoted his magnificent abilities wholly to the service of the people, and given them what, if applied to the advancement of his own interests, would have made him a millionaire many times over. The people everywhere are beginning to thoroughly understand this, and it has made John A. Logan the foremost man in the Republican party, as it will, in all probability make him the foremost man in the Nation in 1888. Nothing but his death can prevent his nomination for President, and almost certain election.

The Indianapolis JOURNAL, May 20, 1885:

The re-election of Senator John A. Logan is a victory worthy to be celebrated with the greatest enthusiasm. The contest had assumed a National character, and the triumph of the man and of the party is only second in importance and influence to the election of a President.

The Chicago TRIBUNE, July 29, 1885:

We wish to call the attention of the readers throughout the State, and of Democrats especially, to the present condition of affairs in the old Sixth Representative District, the one which turned from its evil ways not long ago and sent Weaver to the Legislature and Logan to the United States Senate. Reliable agriculturists from that region frequently visit Chicago, and from them facts of the greatest interest have been secured. We are informed that throughout the counties of Mason, Schuyler, Menard, and Cass—all in the Sixth District before the new apportionment—a degree of prosperity is now felt never before known in the history of the region, and that the crops, when fully garnered, promise to surpass any product of past years. Immediately after the election, corn seemed to take a new start and has attained a remarkable hight, while the ears are now filling out beautifully. To see three or four large ears on one stalk is nothing uncommon, and the total yield will be something enormous. Wheat has thrived equally well; there is less chess in it than formerly, and, in order to learn what a weevil looks like, the farmers have to get down an old Agricultural Department report. Oats, rye, and other small grains are not behind. The potato crop will be something stupendous; the tops fairly cumber the ground, the yield beneath is not less exceptional, and such is the freedom of the plants from insect enemies that as high as 50 cents has been paid in Menard county for a potato-bug as a curiosity. The same exceptional vigor seems to have extended to animal life; Schuyler county calves look like yearlings; there never were such shoats before in Cass, and in Mason some of the mule colts have shown such points that they will be trained for the race-course and the steeplechase instead of the plow. As for chickens and turkeys—well, this season's pullets are laying two eggs a day already, and one thrifty but unscrupulous husbandman is said to have sold a young turkey hatched in March to a circus-man for an ostrich. And so it goes, all over the district. Nature seems to have been in a gracious mood since the special election, and the people of the district are reaping the benefits of her good will. It is scarcely necessary to call attention to the moral. It rests with the people of the counties named to determine whether or not the present state of things shall continue. The responsibility will come upon them again with the next election.

WELCOME TO LOGAN.

BY THE UNION LEAGUE CLUB.

The Union League Club, of Chicago, tendered Gen. Logan a reception which he accepted for the evening of May 26th. The meeting was called to order and President Adams delivered the address of welcome. Gen. Logan was then introduced and responded as follows:

MR. CHAIRMAN AND GENTLEMEN: I would be less than a man if I should fail to appreciate the compliment extended to me on this occasion by the Union League Club of Chicago. This club is an association of gentlemen, whose primary purpose is to aid in the preservation of the integrity of the Union and to promote the prosperity of all the people by an honest administration of the Government. [Applause.] These objects should have the indorsement of every honest citizen, and I hope I may be believed when I declare they are most dear to my own heart. I feel the strongest attachment for my country. My most fervent prayer is for its prosperity and permanence. I have from my earliest manhood exerted my best energies and abilities in its behalf. If in so doing I have failed in any degree in securing the approbation of my fellow-citizens, I have at least the consolation of knowing that the rectitude of my intentions has not thus far been called in question. [Applause.] It is not my purpose to enter into the history or details of our recent Senatorial contest. Neither shall I speak of the trials through which we passed or the perils which were averted. Suffice it to say that the victory is ours. [Applause.] To the steadfastness of our people and the integrity of the Republican representatives in our Legislature is the credit for our success due. [Applause.] I wish to disclaim the idea that the gatherings of people at the different towns and villages along the road from Springfield to Chicago and the grand reception tendered by the people the night of my arrival here or this banquet are considered by me as intended to be personally complimentary to myself, but recognitions of the principles underlying the Republican party for which this contest was made. [Applause.] A contest for a seat in the United States Senate has seldom caused much popular solicitude, but the protracted controversy, the fact that the parties were equally divided, and the loss of members of the Legislature by death—all conspired to bring the contest prominently to the notice of the people throughout the United States. That the opponents of the Republican party had become at this early day tired of the management of National affairs in the hands of their own friends is shown in the fact that they actually staid away from the polls in the Thirty-Fourth Senatorial District [laughter and applause], giving us a majority, so that a Republican might again be chosen to represent the State of Illinois in the United States Senate. [Applause.] This has caused the Republicans throughout the country to discover the turn of the tide in favor of Republican principles, and the hearts of all true patriots to leap with joy. [Applause.] To the energy and fidelity of the Republicans of this district are we indebted for this result. [Applause.]

If I may be permitted to speak of myself in connection with this contest, I will say that I am very much gratified that again I have the honor of representing in the United States Senate this great State with a population of over 3,000,000 intelligent people, with an area of 56,650 square miles, comprising 36,256,000 acres of land, with more miles of railroad than any other State, and a canal that must become a National highway in the future [cheers], whose citizens possess property valued at $3,210,000,000, being the third State in the Union in the production of coal and second in the number of universities and colleges, and occupying the same high place in the number of scholars enrolled at school.

Illinois is varied in its agricultural products, its trade and manufacturing industries, presenting to view a landscape as beautiful as a picture, dotted all over with towns, villages and cities; washed on either side by the two great rivers of our country; with the city of Chicago enthroned on the margin of one of the most beautiful lakes on the continent, possessing a growth, energy, and prosperity which are the marvels of the age. Why should a man not feel a pardonable pride in having been selected as a representative of such a State against combinations of patronage and money, without the influence or use of either? The people of this, my native, State have been more than kind to me in the past. Whether I shall be able to fill the full measure of my public duty my future must disclose. I can only promise that I shall in all things try to be faithful to their great interest and do no act that shall cause them to regret the choice they have just made. [Applause.] That I may be able to satisfy my constituents of the honesty of my intentions and to continue in strict devotion to my duties as one of their representatives is my most ardent desire.

To the members of the Union League Club, Mr. Chairman, through you, I return my thanks, and with a heart full of gratitude I bow to the people of the State of Illinois. [Applause.]